W9-BZD-834

Amazing Animals
Kangaroos

Please visit our Web site, www.garethstevens.com. For a free color catalog of all our high-quality books, call toll free 1-800-542-2595 or fax 1-877-542-2596.

Library of Congress Cataloging-in-Publication Data

Wilsdon, Christina.
  Kangaroos / Christina Wilsdon.
    p. cm. — (Amazing animals)
  Includes index.
  ISBN 978-1-4339-4017-0 (pbk.)
  ISBN 978-1-4339-4018-7 (6-pack)
  ISBN 978-1-4339-4016-3 (library binding)
  1. Kangaroos—Juvenile literature. I. Title.
  QL737.M35W55 2010
  599.2'22—dc22
                                2010008164

This edition first published in 2011 by
Gareth Stevens Publishing
111 East 14th Street, Suite 349
New York, NY 10003

This edition copyright © 2011 Gareth Stevens Publishing.
Original edition copyright © 2006 by Readers' Digest Young Families.

Editor: Greg Roza
Designer: Christopher Logan

Photo credits: Cover, back cover, pp. 4-5, 8-9, 12-13, 20-21, 38-39, 46 Shutterstock.com; pp. 1, 3, 10-11, 16-17, 28-29, 32-33, 44-45 © Digital Vision; pp. 6-7 © iStockphoto.com/Heike Mirabella; p. 13 (bottom) © iStockphoto.com/Michael Sacco; pp. 14-15, 24-25 © Corel Corporation; pp. 18-19, 38 (wallaby) © iStockphoto.com/Gary Unwin; pp. 22-23 © iStockphoto.com/Robert Ahrens; pp. 26-27 © Jupiter Image; pp. 30-31 © iStockphoto.com/Amanda Rohde; p. 33 (top) © Dreamstime.com/Lydia Gartner; pp. 34-35 © Dreamstime.com/Andrew Barker; pp. 36-37 © iStockphoto.com/Marc Prefontaine; p. 39 (tree kangaroo) © iStockphoto.com/Susan Flashman; pp. 42-43 © iStockphoto.com/Flavia Botazzini.

Printed in the United States of America

CPSIA compliance information: Batch #CS10GS: For further information contact Gareth Stevens, New York, New York at 1-800-542-2595.

Amazing Animals
Kangaroos

By Christina Wilsdon

Gareth Stevens
Publishing

Contents

Chapter 1

A Kangaroo Grows Up

Pouch Power

A mother kangaroo is able to tighten the muscles at the top of her pouch to keep her baby safely inside—even when she's hopping at top speed. She relaxes the same muscles to let her baby out.

Baby Kangaroo peeks out from his mother's pouch. He has lived inside the warm pocket ever since he was born. At birth, he was no bigger than a bean. He did nothing but drink Mama Kangaroo's milk. As he drank, his body grew bigger.

Now, Baby Kangaroo is 5 months old. He is big enough to peek at the world outside the pouch. He won't come out for another month. Until then, he will snuggle in the pouch as Mama Kangaroo bounces from place to place searching for grass to eat and shady places to rest. Whenever he pokes his head out, he sees how kangaroos behave.

Kanga Who?

Native Australians—known as Aborigines (aa-buh-RIH-juh-neez)—have lived in Australia for thousands of years. An old story says the kangaroo got its name when a British explorer pointed to a kangaroo and asked an Aborigine what it was called. The man's reply sounded like "kangaroo." For many years, people believed this meant "I don't know" in the Aborigine's language. However, it was actually the tribe's word for one kind of kangaroo.

One day, Baby Kangaroo pops out of the pouch. He takes a few shaky hops. Then he turns around to go back inside Mama Kangaroo's pouch. She relaxes her pouch so it is wide open. Baby Kangaroo slips into the pocket and flips over so his head pokes out in front again. He then curls up his long tail and feet.

Every day, Baby Kangaroo makes a few trips out of the pouch. He grows bigger and stronger. His hops become steadier. Soon he spends longer amounts of time outside the pouch.

Sometimes Baby Kangaroo wanders a little too far away. Then Mama Kangaroo searches for him, clucking loudly. Baby Kangaroo squeaks in reply. He pops back inside her pouch and settles in to drink some milk.

Wild Words

A baby kangaroo is called a joey. A joey that is too big to fit in a pouch is called a young-at-foot. A male kangaroo is called a buck. A female is called a doe. Large male kangaroos are called boomers, and some large females are called fliers.

Easy Lunch

As this mother kangaroo grazes, her joey leans out of her pouch. The joey stretches its neck to nibble on grass, too.

Bath Time

Once a joey leaves the pouch for good, it still spends a lot of time with its mother. The joey frequently presses up against its mother as she grooms it from head to toe.

One day, Baby Kangaroo tries to get back into Mama Kangaroo's pouch—but she pushes him away! He tries again and again. But his mother doesn't lean toward him, and she tightens the opening of her pouch so he can't crawl in. Mama Kangaroo keeps Baby Kangaroo out because he has grown too big for her pouch. She must get her pouch ready to hold a new baby. But she is not trying to drive Baby Kangaroo away. He still needs her to care for him. He also still drinks her milk.

Baby Kangaroo quickly accepts that he must stay outside the pouch now. He hops in circles around his mother. He plays with other young kangaroos. He also likes to tug on Mama Kangaroo's ears.

Someday, Baby Kangaroo will leave his mother's side. He will hop away to find a new place to live. Until then, he will stay with Mama Kangaroo.

Chapter 2

The Body of a Kangaroo

A mother kangaroo makes different kinds of milk. A newborn joey gets rich milk with lots of **nutrients**. The milk for a young-at-foot is less rich.

The Family Feature

There are many **species** of kangaroos. Some species are as tall as an adult human. Some are no bigger than a rabbit. Some live in deserts, some live on rocks, and some live in trees. All kangaroo species have one thing in common—females all have pouches to carry their young. Animals with this special feature are called **marsupials** (mahr-SOO-pee-uhlz). A baby marsupial does most of its developing inside its mother's pouch, rather than inside her body.

Pocket Change

A joey does not look like a kangaroo when it is born. It is pink and hairless. Its eyes are sealed shut. Its front legs look like flippers with claws. Its hind legs are just tiny stumps. A newborn red kangaroo joey is about the size of a jelly bean! It weighs less than 1 ounce (28 g).

As soon as it is born, the tiny joey crawls blindly over its mother's fur to find her pouch. The 6-inch (15-cm) journey takes about 5 minutes. Once inside the pouch, the joey quickly begins nursing. It stays there for up to 4 months as it grows and its body takes shape. Meanwhile, the mother kangaroo may still be caring for an older joey. The young-at-foot does not enter the pouch anymore, but it still sticks its head inside to nurse.

Cooling and Cleaning

A kangaroo's short front legs help it keep cool. A hot kangaroo licks the skin between its paws and elbows. The skin has less hair than other parts of its body. It is also rich in **blood vessels** close to the surface. When a breeze blows over the wet skin, it cools the blood by carrying away extra heat. This helps cool off the kangaroo's whole body.

A kangaroo's front paws are shaped like hands. It uses them to scratch, groom itself, and hold on to plants.

Teeth on the Move

Kangaroos are plant eaters. Some species eat mostly grass. Other kinds, especially the small species, eat mostly leaves. A kangaroo has sharp front teeth for cutting plants. It has six sharp top teeth and two bottom teeth. The bottom teeth press the grass or leaves against a pad on the top of its mouth. The sharp top teeth slice through the plants.

A kangaroo also has strong back teeth, called molars, for grinding food. These teeth get worn down over time. When a worn-out molar falls out of a kangaroo's mouth, the other molars move forward to fill the empty space. A kangaroo is very old by the time it runs out of molars!

A kangaroo cleans itself just like a cat does. It licks its front paws and rubs them over its body to groom its fur.

A kangaroo's powerful hind legs and feet are one-third of its entire body weight.

Big Foot

Scientists call kangaroos "**macropods**." *Macro* means "big," and *pod* means "foot." So a kangaroo is a "bigfoot"! A kangaroo's hind feet are made for motion. Each hind foot has four toes, one of which is very large. This is the main toe a kangaroo uses when it hops. A second, shorter toe helps out. The other two toes are joined together and are not used for hopping. They form a comb that the kangaroo uses to groom its fur.

Small kangaroos that live among rocks have rough pads on their feet to help them grip the ground. A rock wallaby can jump from rock to rock and land on a spot no bigger than a dime without slipping!

Heads Up

Kangaroos are always on the alert for danger. Big kangaroos watch out for human hunters and **dingoes**. Little kangaroos watch out for these **predators**, too. They must also worry about cats, foxes, eagles, snakes, and big lizards.

A kangaroo's big ears turn in all directions. Its sensitive nostrils sniff the air. Its big eyes see all around it, like those of a deer. If a kangaroo senses danger, it thumps a foot on the ground to warn others.

Chapter 3
Kangaroos in Motion

Trying to make a fast getaway, a kangaroo may leap 35 feet (11 m)—about the length of a school bus—in one bound!

Female Fliers

Female kangaroos are smaller and lighter than males, so they are able to hop much faster. That's why they are sometimes called "fliers." They move so fast they look like they are flying!

Hippity-Hop

What can leap 20 feet (6 m) with ease and hop over an 8-foot (2.4-m) fence in a single bound? The world's largest marsupial—the red kangaroo! A kangaroo does not run like other four-legged animals do. Instead, it tucks its forelegs up and bounces along on its hind feet. A kangaroo in motion spends most of its time in the air, touching down only briefly on its big hind toes.

Most kangaroos can easily hop for hours at a speed of about 20 miles (32 km) per hour. When a kangaroo wants to go faster, it makes its hops longer and covers more ground with each hop.

A kangaroo's legs have tough, stretchy cords in them called **tendons**. Tendons attach muscles to bones and act like springs. When a kangaroo lands, the tendons and muscles in its legs **contract** and build up energy. When the kangaroo leaps forward, the "springs" **expand**, and the kangaroo bounces forward. The longer a kangaroo's hop, the more energy it is able to build up for the next hop.

Tails Toil, Too

A kangaroo's tail does a lot of work. Watch a kangaroo hop, and you will see its tail bounce up and down as it moves. Tendons in the top of the tail store energy from its hops just as tendons in the legs do. The tail helps the kangaroo keep its balance as it moves. It acts as a **rudder** when a kangaroo hops, helping it to change direction in midair. The bouncing tail even works like a pump to help the kangaroo breathe quickly as it hops!

The tail also comes in handy when a kangaroo wants to "crawl-walk," or move forward without hopping. First, the kangaroo leans forward and puts its front feet on the ground. Then it puts its tail on the ground behind them. It leans on its front legs and tail as it swings both hind legs forward to take another step.

Don't Walk!

A swimming kangaroo can kick each leg separately. When a kangaroo hops or crawl-walks on land, it always moves its hind legs together. However, a tree kangaroo uses all four feet when it walks along branches or leaps from limb to limb. When it is on the ground, a tree kangaroo hops.

Forward Gear Only

A kangaroo's long, strong tail is so big that it prevents the kangaroo from moving backward.

When a kangaroo stands up, it leans on its tail and uses it like a third leg.

Chapter 4
Kangaroos Together

Wild Words

A group of kangaroos is called a mob.

Kangaroos would rather run than fight. They don't mind sharing their grazing land with sheep, cattle, or other mobs of kangaroos. They don't defend a territory.

The Roo Crew

A kangaroo mob may have as few as three kangaroos or as many as 100. A mob does not have a leader. It seems to be just a gathering of kangaroos that happen to live in the same area. Kangaroos that live in forests tend to live alone, except when they are raising young.

Even though mobs do not have leaders, some male kangaroos boss around other males. Scientists call them the dominant kangaroos. A dominant male kangaroo may try to keep other males away from the females.

Kangaroos that live on Australia's grassy plains often form mobs. Being in a mob helps keep a kangaroo safe because there are many eyes, ears, and noses to be on the alert for danger. If a predator startles the mob, the kangaroos flee in all directions. This explosion of hopping may confuse the predator so much that it cannot catch a single kangaroo!

Take That!

Most of the time, kangaroos live quietly. They rest during the heat of the day and feed at night when it is cool. Sometimes, however, male kangaroos turn into kick boxers! A male may fight to show that he is dominant. The dominant male is the one who will mate with the females. Fights often break out when a female is ready to mate. Kangaroo fighting is called **sparring**.

Before a male starts sparring, he threatens another male. The threat is a warning that means "scram!" A gray kangaroo sends his warning by pulling up grass or scraping the ground, then rubbing his chest on the scraped area. A red kangaroo may strut around another male while keeping his side turned toward the rival.

If this doesn't chase the other male away, the kangaroo stands up tall and punches at the other male with his forelegs. If the other male punches back, the two begin boxing with their front paws. They also lean back on their tails, lift their hind legs, and kick at each other's bellies. The fight ends when one kangaroo gives up and goes away.

Beware!

This husky red kangaroo buck shows off his muscular body every chance he can. It's his way of letting other males know that he is the dominant kangaroo.

Sparring kangaroos protect their eyes by twisting their heads away from the action.

A mother kangaroo raises her joeys without any help. The joeys are either in her pouch or near her all day and all night.

Kangaroo Families

Male kangaroos do not have pouches, and they do not help females raise the joeys. But a kangaroo doe is up for the job. She may even have three babies of different ages all at the same time. The oldest baby hops at her heels. Tucked inside her pouch is a younger joey. The third is inside her body and has not yet been born. It will not grow big enough to be born until the joey in her pouch is out and about.

How long a joey stays with its mother depends on which kind of kangaroo it is. A red kangaroo joey stays with its mother for a year and a half. A black-striped wallaby baby stays with its mother for less than a year.

Walla-Walla-Who?

Some species of kangaroos are known as wallaroos and wallabies. Wallaroos look like the familiar red and gray kangaroos but are slightly smaller. Wallabies are smaller still. Larger wallabies look like kangaroos, but they are thicker and have more fur.

Chapter 5
Kangaroos in the World

Red kangaroos, the tallest species, live in dry areas and have to travel long distances for food and water.

Kangaroo Cousins

Wallabies are smaller than the great kangaroos. Some wallabies look like their larger cousins and live in grassy woodlands. This yellow-footed rock wallaby lives among rocks and looks different from other wallabies.

Kinds of Kangaroos

About 55 different species of kangaroos hop around in Australia and on the nearby island of New Guinea. They are all part of the macropod family. The six biggest macropods are sometimes called the "great kangaroos." The western gray kangaroo is one of the six. It lives in dry **scrublands** and forests. It grazes at night and rests under trees during the day. The other great kangaroos are the eastern gray kangaroo, the red kangaroo, and three species of wallaroos.

Scientists place species called rat-kangaroos, potoroos, and bettongs in a related but separate family, called potoroids (paht-uh-ROYDZ). They look more like **rodents** than kangaroos!

Climbing Roos

Tree kangaroos live in rain forests. A tree kangaroo's front legs are almost as long as its back legs. But its hind feet are not enormous like other kangaroos' feet are. It walks easily along branches as it looks for leaves to eat. Once on the ground, it hops.

Kangaroos at Home

Australia and New Guinea boast many kinds of **habitats**, from deserts to rain forests. Over time, kangaroos and their relatives have adapted to almost every habitat. Red kangaroos live in dry places and grasslands with a few shady trees. Gray kangaroos live in woodlands that have some open space for grazing. Some Australians call gray kangaroos "foresters" because they live among trees.

Steep rock cliffs in deserts are home to rock wallabies, which get all the water they need from the plants they eat. The tree kangaroo, however, is adapted to the rain forest. Even its fur is parted so that rain funnels off its back instead of into its face.

Fast Facts About Red Kangaroos

Scientific name	*Macropus rufus*
Class	Mammals
Order	Diprotodontia
Size	Males up to 6 feet (1.8 m) tall
	Females up to 4 feet (1.2 m) tall
Weight	Males to 200 pounds (91 kg)
	Females to 70 pounds (32 kg)
Life span	18 years in the wild
	25 years in captivity
Habitat	Dry grasslands near scattered trees
Top speed	About 30 miles (48 km) per hour

Where Kangaroos Live

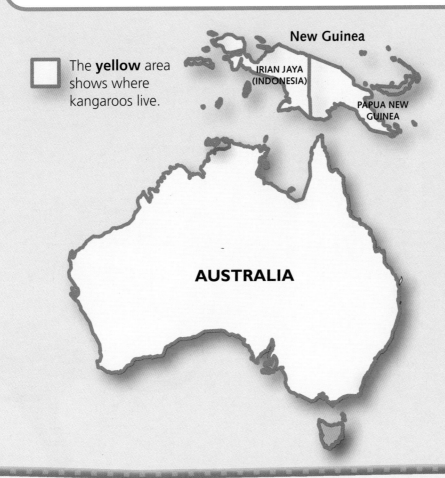

☐ The **yellow** area shows where kangaroos live.

New Guinea

IRIAN JAYA
(INDONESIA)

PAPUA NEW
GUINEA

AUSTRALIA

Marsupials Galore!

More than 100 species of marsupials live in Australia and the islands around it. Kangaroos, koala bears, Tasmanian devils, opossums, and other species live there and nowhere else in the world! The Virginia opossum is the only marsupial in North America.

There are so many kangaroos in Australia that kangaroo-crossing signs are posted along roads to warn drivers to be on the alert. These signs are even posted in the suburbs of large cities.

The Future of Kangaroos

Millions of red and gray kangaroos live in Australia. Aborigines have always hunted them for food. When Europeans arrived in the 1600s, they hunted kangaroos, too. But when Europeans started farming in Australia, kangaroos took food and water intended for sheep. Farmers began shooting large numbers of kangaroos.

Today, red and gray kangaroos are still hunted to control their population. This hunt is controlled by law. The kangaroos' meat is used for food and their skins for leather.

Many small kangaroo species are **endangered**. The cutting of rain forests removes habitat for tree kangaroos. Cats and foxes, brought to Australia by Europeans, often kill small kangaroos. Today, some small species live only in protected areas. Many people are working to help endangered kangaroos by protecting their habitat.

Glossary

blood vessel—a small tube in an animal's body that carries blood

contract—to get smaller and tighter

dingo—a wild Australian dog with a reddish brown coat

endanger—at risk of dying out

expand—to get larger and looser

habitat—the natural environment where an animal or plant lives

macropod—a marsupial with big back legs and feet

marsupial—a mammal whose young develop inside a pouch on the mother's belly

nutrient—something needed for growth and health

predator—an animal that hunts and eats other animals to survive

rodent—a small animal with large front teeth used for gnawing

rudder—something used like the part that helps steer a boat or plane

scrubland—an area covered with little vegetation

sparring—fighting between kangaroos

species—a category of living things that are the same kind

tendon—a band of tough tissue that connects muscles and bones

Kangaroos: Show What You Know

How much have you learned about kangaroos? Grab a piece of paper and a pencil and write your answers down.

1. What is a joey that is too big to fit in its mother's pouch called?

2. What feature do all marsupials have in common?

3. A kangaroo's back legs and feet make up what amount of its body weight?

4. What does the word *macropod* mean?

5. What is a kangaroo's top speed?

6. What is a group of kangaroos called?

7. What is a male kangaroo that bosses around other males called?

8. How long does a red kangaroo joey stay with its mother?

9. In what parts of the world do kangaroos live?

10. Why are many smaller species of kangaroos endangered?

1. Young-at-foot 2. The females all have pouches to carry their young 3. One-third 4. "Big foot" 5. About 20 miles (32 km) per hour 6. A mob 7. A dominant kangaroo 8. A year and a half 9. Australia and New Guinea 10. Cutting of rain forests removes habitat for tree kangaroos; cats and foxes often hunt small kangaroos

For More Information

Books

Braidich, Shelby. *Kangaroos in the Land Down Under*. New York, NY: Rosen Publishing, 2005.

Montgomery, Sy. *Quest for the Tree Kangaroo: An Expedition to the Cloud Forest of New Guinea*. Boston, MA: Houghton Mifflin, 2009.

Stefoff, Rebecca. *The Marsupia! Order*. New York, NY: Marshall Cavendish Benchmark, 2008.

Web Sites

Kangaroo
animal.discovery.com/mammals/kangaroo
Find facts about kangaroos and videos of the animals in action.

Red Kangaroo
animals.nationalgeographic.com/animals/mammals/red-kangaroo.html
Read interesting facts about red kangaroos and see photos, with links to other Australian animals.

Index